TELLING TALES

...tock remembers

Enid

Bl

Other authors in the *Telling Tales* series:

Theresa Breslin, Gillian Cross, Anne Fine

Michelle Magorian, Michael Morpurgo

Jenny Nimmo

Gillian Baverstock is Enid Blyton's elder daughter. Before her marriage she worked in children's publishing. Then she taught infants and juniors for 25 years, before returning to publishing with the family company that ran the Enid Blyton copyrights. She has recently been co-writing a children's magazine called Blue Moon and talking to schools about books, creative writing, the imagination and, of course, Enid Blyton.

Sh███1's
book██1 in
1958 ██d is
███

ISBN 0 7497 4275 5

A CIP catalogue record for this title is available from the British Library.

Printed and bound in Great Britain by Cox and Wyman Ltd, Reading, Berks.

Contents

Gillian Baverstock remembers Enid Blyton

Enid Blyton's Books

Born in 1897, Enid Blyton wrote more than 700 books and is one of the most prolific, widely translated and avidly read of all children's writers. She was married with two daughters, and died in 1968.

In 1951, in answer to the many questions that children asked in their letters to her, Enid Blyton wrote *The Story of My Life*. I hope that by using her own recollections and quoting her exact words where possible, this *Telling Tales* reveals something of the vibrant, amusing and thoughtful person that I knew.

Gillian Baverstock

Enid Blyton

Her family and her childhood

Thomas Carey Blyton and his wife, Theresa, had moved from Sheffield to London to join his brothers in their uncle's firm selling Yorkshire cloth. Enid, my mother, was born on 11th August 1897, in a small flat above a shop in Dulwich.

The following year, the family moved to Beckenham where Enid lived throughout her childhood. Her two brothers, Hanly and Carey, were born here in 1899 and 1902.

The Blyton family home in Beckenham.

An Irish grandmother

Enid's grandparents still lived in Sheffield where they

had raised their seven children. Thomas Carey was their fourth child. When Enid and her brothers were young, they spent Christmas at their uncle's house in Sheffield where their Blyton grandparents came to join the celebrations.

Enid was fascinated by her grandmother. Mary Ann Hanly was the daughter of an Irish doctor and very well-educated. Enid remembered her as a little old lady with bright eyes, a vivacious smile and a fund of amusing sayings. She sat in the chimney corner surrounded by her grandchildren, sometimes singing old Irish songs to them, sometimes bewitching them with her stories of leprechauns and banshees. My mother was sure that the talent for music that came out in the next three

generations of the Blyton family, as well as her own gift for story-telling, was inherited from her Irish ancestors.

Thomas Carey Blyton (left)

Enid had a very close relationship with her father. It began when she was a baby, so ill with whooping cough that the doctor thought she could not survive the night. Her father rocked her in his arms until dawn when, to his joy, he realised that his baby daughter was sleeping peacefully.

From the time that she could walk, Enid accompanied her father everywhere. In the early years of the 20th century, Beckenham was surrounded by unspoilt country which they explored together. Her father loved wildlife and nature and taught her everything he knew, giving her a knowledge and love of the subject that never left her.

A garden

Enid's father was a keen gardener and helped her prepare her first patch of garden when she was five. She wanted to grow plants from seeds, so he made a bargain with her. 'If you want anything badly, you have to work for it,' he said. 'I will give you enough money to buy your own seeds, if you earn it.' So Enid cleaned his bicycle beautifully, and weeded a large flower bed very carefully, earning six pennies that bought her six packets of seeds. She cared for them with her father's help and they all grew and flowered. She never forgot the excitement of that summer, and all through her life gardening, even weeding, was a great pleasure. Soon after her marriage, she and Hugh, her husband, moved into a newly-built house and created a garden out of a field. The little pond set with crazy paving is still there today, restored by the present owners who found the old crazy paving under the lawn.

Animals

Enid loved animals and longed for a pet, but her father did not want a dog or a cat spoiling his garden, and her mother felt exactly the same about her house. Enid kept caterpillars, but she couldn't grow fond of them, though she found them interesting, and liked 'feeling their funny little clingy feet' walking over her hand.

She brought home a lost kitten one evening, knowing that her parents must not find out. She kept it in a shed at the bottom of the garden and, helped by Annie, their young maid, she managed to keep it a secret for two weeks. She came home from school one day and was heart-broken to be told by Annie that her mother had discovered the kitten and got rid of it. Years later, Enid made up for the pets that she had longed for, filling her house and garden with birds and animals of all kinds.

Music

Her father's other great passion was music. His sister was a concert pianist and he also played the piano very well. Enid wrote: 'One of the things I remember most clearly about my childhood is lying in bed at night, and hearing my father playing Beethoven's sonatas, Chopin's nocturnes and ballades, grand pieces from Liszt and Rachmaninoff, and a great deal of Mozart. I knew them by heart. . . and now, whenever I hear those same pieces of music played, I seem to be back in my little bed, almost asleep, hearing my father playing hour after hour downstairs, all those years ago.'

A gift for music?

When Enid was six years old, her father gave her her first piano lesson. She was quick to learn and had a good touch. Her father was sure that, like her aunt, whom she resembled in looks, she would become a professional musician. From that time until she was nearly 19, when

**Enid's aunt,
the concert pianist.**

she gained a place at the Guildhall School of Music, her future was mapped out, with piano practice gradually using up her spare time as she grew older.

When my sister Imogen and I were young, my mother sang songs and carols for us, and played the settings for her own songs, especially those by her nephew Carey Blyton (the creator of *Bananas in Pyjamas*), but she never played the piano for pleasure, as she described her father playing. Perhaps the never-ending piano practice throughout her childhood had destroyed for her the joy of music.

First school

There was a small school across the road from the Blytons' house in Beckenham and Enid and her brothers started their education there. She enjoyed reading, English, nature, art and music, but maths was beyond her and she hated it.

Reading

Enid was a very keen reader from a young age. She wrote: 'The book I loved best as a young child . . . was *The Princess and The Goblin* by George Macdonald. It wasn't so much the story as the strange "feel" of the tale, the "atmosphere" . . . It hung over me for a very long time, and gave me pleasant shivers.' She enjoyed Lewis Carroll's *Alice's Adventures in Wonderland* which she found very funny, and *Coral Island* by R.M. Ballantyne because it was so exciting, 'and set me off dreaming of adventures of all kinds'. Anna Sewell's *Black Beauty* was a favourite although she found some parts very sad, and she read *Little Women* by Louisa M. Alcott again and again because the children were so real.

Poetry

She was fond of poetry, although she admitted that she did not always understand it, but she added: '. . . the lilt of the words and the beautiful stringing-together of lines lifted my heart. My father used to quote poetry so often that it became part of my life.'

A love of books

Her father was self-educated but was very well-read, with a wide knowledge of many subjects. As a young man, he had built up a library by buying a 'sixpenny classic' every week and had since greatly extended it. It delighted him to find that his daughter shared his love of reading and, by the time she was ten, she was borrowing books from his shelves.

Enid devoured every book her father owned, which included her first French book that she had to read with a dictionary beside her since she knew no French. Her father finally found her reading an unsuitable German novel, helped by a dictionary again, and was so horrified that he locked up his bookcases!

Family problems

When Enid was ten she moved to St Christopher's School for Girls in Beckenham. She made new friends easily and thoroughly enjoyed the opportunities for playing lacrosse and tennis, swimming – and learning French properly.

St Christopher's School, Beckenham. Enid is seated third from the right on the third row.

Theresa Blyton

The Blyton family moved to a new and bigger house but the relationship between Enid's parents was deteriorating. Enid had never got on very well with her mother, Theresa, who favoured her two sons and insisted that Enid help with the cooking and housework while the boys were allowed to play. Her mother felt it was her duty to bring up her daughter to manage a home and family and was particularly annoyed when her husband took Enid off to do other things. Enid, of course, was only too happy to escape the hated chores.

Her unhappiest time

By the time Enid was 12, her parents were constantly arguing and Enid could measure her father's anger by the volume and fierceness of his piano playing later in the evening. Finally, in 1910, matters came to a head, and after a tremendous row her father walked out.

Barbara Stoney, Enid Blyton's official biographer, read through all her books and found in *The Six Bad Boys* a piece which seemed so like what must have happened in the Blyton household that she read it to Enid's brother, Hanly. He was very moved and confirmed that, apart from changing the sex of the three children involved, it was a true report of what had occurred. Until then, no one in the family was aware that Enid had recorded her own experience in her fictional books.

Extract from *The Six Bad Boys* – from chapters 8 and 11

> [The children were] *huddled together on the top stairs, listening . . . shivering . . . partly with cold, partly with fear. These dreadful rows! They all put their arms round one another for warmth. . .*
> *He [their father] spoke in a quiet voice. 'This is the*

end. It's not good for any of us to go on like this. I am sure that you are right when you say that I am to blame for everything. So I'm going. Then perhaps you will be happier, all of you.'...

The front door slammed. The front gate clicked shut. Quick footsteps went down the lane, and then faded away... He did not come back...

That was a dreadful time for the three children. They had to cope with a tearful, ... angry mother, who had no idea where her husband was. They had to promise her not to tell anyone their father had gone away because of a row. They had to say he was gone on a visit. They had to face the fact that perhaps their father might never come back again.

Reality

Enid's father had recently started up his own business as a clothing wholesaler, and he had found it difficult to cope with the constant nagging and criticism from his wife, especially over his favouring of Enid. Also, he had met an intelligent woman who shared his love of books and music which his wife had never done, wrapped up as

11

she was in domesticity. Enid, although she does not mention it in *The Six Bad Boys*, was shattered to hear that her father had taken someone else into his life. She felt guilty that she had so often been the focus of her parents' rows, but also hurt that her closeness to her father was not enough to prevent him leaving.

Enid's mother refused to divorce her husband. The children were forbidden to tell anyone what had really happened, so Enid could not seek comfort from her friends. The family moved to a house at the other end of town, and Enid began to see her father again, although he never visited her at home. They would walk into the country on fine days, or go to the theatre or the cinema. When Enid grew older, she visited his office and he took her to the London theatres which they both enjoyed. But nothing could make up for what had happened. She had lost her dearest friend; occasional meetings could never replace the happy daily companionship they had shared.

Growing up

Enid, now 13, threw herself into life at school, especially sport. She and her friends formed an entertainment

St Christopher's lacrosse team. Enid is second from the right on the back row.

group, for which she wrote items and played the piano. She and two friends started a magazine – Enid wrote the stories, and the other two provided the poems and illustrations. She was known for the tricks she played in class, some probably taught to her by her brothers who were at boarding school.

In 1913, Mademoiselle Bertaine, her French teacher, invited Enid to stay with her family in Annecy, a small French town set by a beautiful lake and surrounded by mountains. Years later, her French teacher became Mam'zelle Abominable in the first book of the St Clare's series *The Twins at St Clare's*. She was exactly like the character in the book: warm hearted, hot tempered, larger than life, unforgettable!

An exciting moment

My mother not only read Arthur Mee's *Children's Encyclopaedia* from cover to cover several times, but she also took his weekly magazine. When she was nearly 14 she entered a poetry competition and to her 'utter amazement and delight' he wrote to her: 'You can write. Send in other things to our page. Perhaps one day you will *really* write.' She waited eagerly for the next magazine: 'When my little poem was printed on the children's page in the magazine I could have cried for joy! My words seemed quite different when they were printed, not written – they seemed so much more important.'

Night stories

As a little girl, stories filled Enid's mind just before she went to sleep. She did not make them up, they were just there. She called them her 'night stories'. Later, she told stories to her younger brothers, especially during the time of the family rows. She loved writing of all kinds –

poems, stories, her diary, letters. She said: 'My family didn't even know that I *wanted* to write, nor did they know that I could. And, if you are a child . . . you can't say, "But I *know* I must write" . . . [especially as] they thought that my gift . . . was music . . . But I was not a composer. I could only interpret other people's music and I wanted to create something of my own – not music, but books.'

Learning her craft

Enid began to read biographies of authors and books on the art of writing, and every night in her attic bedroom she wrote stories, poems and articles for adults which she sent to different publishers. Her mother grew very impatient with her for this waste of her time, especially when she should have been practising the piano; and for the waste of money on the stamps and packaging. Enid began creeping downstairs early to get to the post first, to retrieve the returned manuscripts before any family came downstairs.

A sympathetic ear

Enid would have become very discouraged but for one adult who understood her. Mary Attenborough, who eventually became a well-known artist, was Enid's closest friend. Mary's aunt, Mabel Attenborough, was the Sunday school teacher at the Baptist Church which Enid attended. Mabel Attenborough knew Enid well since the two girls spent much time together, and it was she in whom Enid confided her ambition to become a writer. Mabel Attenborough's encouragement over the next few years enabled the young girl to persevere with her writing in the face of constant rejection. Enid left school in 1915, and spent the next year studying singing, harmony and piano. She passed her LRAM (Licentiate of the Royal Academy of Music) – a major music exam – and was offered a place at the Guildhall School of Music just before she was 19.

Decisions

In spite of this success, Enid knew that she could not follow the musical path her father had planned for her. Apart from her early poem, none of her writing had been accepted for publication, but she was certain she was meant to write. In the meantime, however, she had to earn her own living somehow. Mabel Attenborough asked friends of hers if Enid could stay with them for a few weeks while she decided her future. So Enid was invited to join the Hunt family who farmed near Ipswich. My mother loved the life on the farm and helped with all the farmwork. The Hunts' daughter, Ida, was a trainee teacher at Ipswich Girls' High School and, having watched Enid teaching children at Sunday school, suggested she should take up teaching and write during the holidays. So Enid made enquiries and was offered a place as an apprentice teacher in the school's kindergarten.

No more music!

However, there were forms her father needed to sign and she was fearful of what his reaction would be to her giving up music. She plucked up her courage and telephoned him. He was astounded at her change of plan, but he thought teaching was a very worthwhile career and that it would end her idea of becoming a writer. Enid was amazed he had given in so easily, but later remembered that, when she was eight, she had been examined by a phrenologist – a scientist who tries to assess a person's abilities by examining the size and shape of their skull.

Her father had expected to be told that she was a musical genius, but the phrenologist had said that she was a born teacher. So he had accepted her decision without argument because of that long-ago forecast.

The teacher

Enid joined Ipswich Girls' High School that September. She loved the school, the children, and the teaching. She

found both her artistic and musical abilities very helpful and soon began to write and illustrate some of the work she used with the children. She found time for her own work, too, and had several poems published.

In December 1919, aged 22, Enid became a certificated Froebel teacher. She joined a boys' boarding school at Bickley Park, but found she had little time for writing. In January 1921, at

Enid, aged 20.

Mabel Attenborough's suggestion, Enid became a governess with the Thompson family, whose four boys were recovering from diphtheria. During her time there, more children from neighbouring families came to join her class, which eventually numbered 14.

My mother enjoyed those years: she loved the children and wrote everything they used in class, but, more than this, her writing career was taking off. Her first book was published in 1922, a book of poems called *Child Whispers*. It was a collection of poems written for her class. I met one of the class in 1997, who told me that no poem went into that book unless it had been approved by every one of her pupils.

The writer and educationalist

Enid's work for adults was being accepted by many publications including *The Poetry Review* and *The Strand Magazine*, and in 1922 she earned £200 from her writing. But after several years of teaching, Enid realised she wanted to write for children and she turned her back on the adult market.

The importance of children

My mother was surrounded by children all day long, and they became more interesting to her than anything else.

She learned how to tell a story for different ages, how to use humour to the best effect, the importance of pace and dialogue, and the different kinds of story that children enjoy. She wrote: 'It was the children themselves who taught me how to write. . . No adult can teach you that as they can.'

The educationalist

In 1923, Enid was engaged to write a column for *The Teacher's World*, a weekly journal taken by most primary

Enid, aged 26.

schools. By 1929, she was writing a page containing schemes of work for teachers and stories and poems for children. Her work in *The Teacher's World* and in *Sunny Stories*, a weekly magazine that she was writing at the same time, made her name known to children everywhere, long before any of her children's 'novels' were published. By the mid 20s, she was receiving up to a hundred letters a week from children telling her which stories they had enjoyed most and why.

In the next few years, the greater part of her output was educational, including nature, religion, stories, poems, songs and plays, often in the form of school readers compiled from her work in *The Teacher's World*. She also edited three different sets of encyclopaedia for teachers in junior and infant schools.

Marriage

In August 1924, Enid married Major Hugh Pollock, the new editor of the book department of George Newnes Ltd. He had been a professional soldier, and was awarded the DSO (Distinguished Service Order) in 1919. They had met when discussing some educational nature books which Newnes were to publish.

Enid and Hugh lived in a flat in London for a year before moving to the country. He encouraged her writing, and was very helpful over contracts and royalties as more publishers became interested in her work, and was happy for her to use the name 'Blyton' professionally. They divorced in 1942 and both remarried in 1943. My mother's second husband was Kenneth Darrell Waters, a London surgeon and a keen athlete.

Old Thatch in Bourne End.

First stories

In 1929 Enid and Hugh moved to Old Thatch in Bourne End where I was born in 1931 and Imogen in 1935. By the end of 1937, my mother had published 16 storybooks that were *not* aimed at the school market: Christmas annuals, collections of short stories, or of stories about the same characters, like *The Green Goblin Book* and *The Yellow Fairy Book*, first written for *Sunny Stories* or *The Teachers' World*.

The children's author

My mother wrote her first 'novel' in 1936 when I was five, and *The Adventures of the Wishing Chair* is perfect for a young reader. Other books soon followed: *Mr*

Galliano's Circus and *Secret Island*, *The Treasure Hunters* and *The Naughtiest Girl in the School*. I used to read chapters of her latest book hot from the typewriter after school, impatient for the next day's instalment. Fortunately, my mother was a very fast writer!

Well-known series

Throughout the 40s and 50s Enid Blyton wrote 13 series of books for older children: adventure stories, school stories, mystery stories, magical stories, circus stories and farming stories. There were at least 13 other series for younger children, ranging from comic-strip books (Mary Mouse), through story collections (Amelia Jane), to Noddy and Bom. She also published a number of stand-alone books like *The Boy Next Door* or *Smuggler Ben*.

The character Amelia Jane was based on a large hand-made doll given to me on my third birthday. My mother used her as a very naughty puppet to entertain my friends when they came to tea, until we rolled on the floor, laughing helplessly at her tricks and bad behaviour. So my mother wrote enough stories for three books about Amelia Jane and the chaos she created amongst the toys.

A new magazine

My mother finished writing for *Teachers' World* in 1945.
In 1952 she ended her work for *Sunny Stories*, and in

November that year launched *The Enid Blyton Magazine* which followed the same format but also included reports of the clubs that she ran for children in aid of different charities.

Enid with her two daughters, Gillian (back) and Imogen (front), in 1946.

Answering letters

In the 50s she worked very hard but refused to have a secretary, although she used a typist if she needed work copied. But her daily postbag was enormous now, and to ease the burden she agreed to use postcards with a printed message that she could sign. These had pictures of the Famous Five, the Secret Seven and Noddy on them, and enabled her to acknowledge letters that did not need a long reply.

Published abroad

After the war, Enid Blyton books appeared in all the

English-speaking countries, and in 1947 The Boys' Clubs of America awarded *The Island of Adventure* the prize for the best junior book published that year. During the 50s many of her books were translated into all the European languages. Today, her books are published in nearly 50 languages.

Beyond books

In the 50s, Noddy became very popular and Enid found herself preparing scripts for Noddy records and TV. She wrote *Noddy in Toyland*, a musical play, and another play, *The Famous Five*. Both of these were produced at Christmas for a number of years. She carefully checked every design for Noddy merchandise just as she had always checked every piece of artwork for her books. She supervised scripts for two Famous Five stories filmed for Saturday children's cinema. All this on top of the enormous output of books – not just the writing, but also the overseeing of compilations of old work – began to take their toll on her boundless energy.

A wooden figure of Noddy presented to Enid in 1957 by David White of Sampson Low publishers.

Daily routine

Enid Blyton wrote more than 700 books in the 40 years between 1922 and 1962. From the beginning, she wrote to a routine. In the 20s and 30s, she usually wrote only in the morning. However, as her work increased in the 40s and 50s she worked all day when she was writing a novel, although she took time off to visit London or to play golf. She never worked at weekends and as little as possible on holiday. Every day, she had to find time to correct proofs, check artwork and answer her many letters.

Writing books

Children were constantly asking Enid Blyton how she wrote her books, and she explained that she used two different methods of writing. Educational work, nature

Enid Blyton talking to some of her fans.

and religious books needed careful research and planning; poetry needed careful thought. On the other hand, her stories were drawn directly from her imagination. She said that this kind of writing was like watching the story on a cinema screen, while she typed as fast as she could to keep up with the action and dialogue.

Where do stories come from?

In a letter to Dr Peter McKellar who was researching a book *Imagination and Thinking*, Enid Blyton explained that, before she started to write, she knew the type of book she had to write and its length. Then: 'I shut my eyes for a few minutes, with my portable typewriter on my knee – I make my mind a blank and wait – and then, as clearly as I would see real children, my characters stand before me in my mind's eye. I see them in detail – hair, eyes, feet, clothes, expression. . . More than that, I know their characters. . . They take on movement and life – they talk and laugh (I hear them) and perhaps I see that one of them has a dog, or a parrot. . . Then behind the characters appears the setting, in colour, of course, of an old house – a ruined castle – an island – a row of houses.

'That's enough for me and . . . I begin. The first sentence comes straight into my mind, I don't have to think of it – I don't have to think of anything.'

She explained this further in *The Story of My Life*: 'The story comes out complete and whole from beginning to the end. . . If I tried to think out or invent the whole book, I could not do it. For one thing, it would bore me, and for another, it would lack the "verve" and the extraordinary touches and surprising ideas that flood out from my imagination. People in my books make jokes I could never have thought of myself. I am merely a sightseer, a reporter, and interpreter.'

Imagination

Imagination was for Enid Blyton the vital ingredient in her writing. She said in her autobiography: 'It is open to all writers to enrich their imagination and to make it easy of access. The more one observes and hears and learns, the more one reads, and ponders and muses consciously on this, that and the other, the richer the imagination becomes.'

My mother did not consciously use people or places in her stories, but after she had written a book, she might be reminded of a person she had known or a place she had seen. In another letter to Dr Peter McKellar, she says: '. . . I think my imagination contains all the things I have ever seen or heard, things my conscious mind has long forgotten – and they have all been jumbled about till a light penetrates into the mass, and a happening here or an object there is taken out, transmuted, or formed into something that takes a natural and rightful place in the story – I may recognise it or I may not – I don't think that I use anything I have not seen or experienced – I don't think I could. . . Our books are facets of ourselves.'

She told her agent that she realised that George in the Famous Five was a reflection of herself as a child, longing to be like her brothers. Loony, the spaniel in the Barney Books, was definitely our last dog and Kiki came from her aunt's clever parrot. The Famous Five books are usually set in Dorset where she went on holiday three times a year, and the setting for the Mystery books of the Five Find-Outers is the countryside near the Thames where we lived during the 30s.

Pleasures

Though Enid Blyton led a very busy life, she enjoyed many of the things that she had loved as a child. Books were always very important to her and she read every night in bed and at the weekend. She read modern fiction, detective stories, biography and other non-fiction.

Enid off to play golf.

Although I remember her loving tennis and swimming when I was a child, in the 50s, she only played golf which she and Kenneth, her second husband, both enjoyed.

She loved the theatre and cinema as a girl and a young woman but Kenneth had had his hearing damaged at the Battle of Jutland and was very deaf. They occasionally went to the theatre but musicals were really all that he could enjoy.

She adored being involved in the theatre when *Noddy in Toyland* and *The Famous Five* were produced, and attended rehearsals and performances as often as she could. She was basically a shy person, and found the world of the theatre fascinating and theatre people amusing and very easy to be with.

Her great love was always her garden and the wildlife around her. She used to work outside in the summer and the birds grew to know her. Several became so tame they would take crumbs from her hand. She loved the beauty of the Purbeck Hills in Dorset where she used to sit on the hillside overlooking Poole harbour, listening to the larks singing as she answered letters or corrected proofs while Kenneth played golf.

The last years

My mother was physically very fit, and she remarked once that if she faced ill-health when she was old, she prayed she would be affected physically not mentally. Unfortunately, in the early 60s she began to suffer from Alzheimer's disease (a disease that affects people's memory). She was unable to write anything after 1963 and her last three books were published the following year. I remember her saying to me at that time: 'I'm finding it so difficult to read now, because I can't remember what I've just read.' She died in her sleep of a heart attack in November 1968, when she could still recognise people close to her and remember something of her past.

Gillian Baverstock

2000

Enid Blyton's Books
An overview by Sheila Ray

ENID BLYTON was born with a gift for storytelling. She told stories to her younger brothers and to friends at school and soon began to write them down. She also wrote poetry and her first published work was a poem, 'Have you. . .?', which appeared in *Nash's Magazine* in 1917. Even her first published book was a collection of poems, *Child Whispers* (1922). She chose teaching as a career because she thought it would be a good way of learning about children and the sort of stories they enjoy, but she could not have guessed, in her wildest dreams, how large an audience she would eventually reach.

Child Whispers

The secret of success

For much of the 20th century Enid Blyton was the most popular children's writer, famous throughout the world. In 1974 she was listed as the fourth most translated author, with only

Lenin, Marx and Jules Verne ahead of her. One reason for her popularity is that she wrote for children of all ages. They begin by listening to tales about Noddy and other nursery characters and go on to read the fantasy, adventure and family stories for themselves while girls often go on reading her books for longer than boys because the school stories about St Clare's and Malory Towers appeal to them.

The main reason for Enid Blyton's popularity, however, is her skill in creating exciting plots and interesting characters, and then telling the stories in such a way that the reader wants to find out what happens next. Some of her skill may be due to the fact that for many years she produced a magazine, *Sunny Stories*, which appeared weekly or fortnightly. This contained short stories, a picture story for younger children, an episode of a serial story, a poem or riddle and a letter to readers in which she seemed to be talking personally to each of them. Her wish to encourage children to buy the next issue of the magazine meant that each episode of the serial story had to finish at an exciting point – what would happen next? Often the characters were in an awkward or dangerous situation or were about to make an important discovery. Who could resist the temptation to find out? When the serials were published as full-length books, the fact that most of the chapters end on a high note helped

Sunny Stories

to make the stories very readable. Enid Blyton had trained herself in the same way that Charles Dickens had done a hundred years before. Both of them published stories in instalments and had to make their readers keen to buy the next one. In the days before television, they were providing the kind of popular entertainment that soap operas do today.

Some of the short stories in *Sunny Stories* were about characters who appeared regularly, so children came to know Amelia Jane the doll, little Betsy-May, foolish Mr Meddle and cunning Brer Rabbit, and wanted to learn more about them too. Enid Blyton and her publishers soon realised that there was a market for sequels and series. Partly because of her letters to readers in *Sunny Stories*, children used to write to her to tell her which stories they most enjoyed and she responded by producing another tale about the same characters.

In the 1930s and 1940s Enid Blyton's popularity was helped by the fact that many teachers and parents regarded her work very favourably. Teachers knew her name through her contributions to their magazine, *Teachers' World*, for which she began to write in the early 1920s, while parents thought that *Sunny Stories* was much better reading for their children than the comics and story-papers which circulated at that time. Today there are grandparents and even great grandparents who enjoyed Enid Blyton's stories when they were children and are pleased to see their grandchildren enjoying them too.

Criticisms

It is important to remember that Enid Blyton was born in 1897, over a hundred years ago, and grew up in a world very different from the one in which we live now. People tend to be influenced for life by the ideas and conditions that are common when they are young. Before World War II, which began in 1939, when Enid Blyton was already over 40, there were few people from other ethnic groups living in Britain. People were more conscious of class differences and children's books usually looked at events from a middle-class point of view. Males and females had clear-cut roles. Boys were expected to be brave and adventurous and do things with their fathers, while girls were encouraged to play with dolls and help their mothers around the house. The average family consisted of a father and mother and two or three children. In the 1930s the British Empire was a major force in the world. All this influenced the way in which Enid Blyton wrote. Her books are still popular, long after they were first published, but attitudes have changed and she is sometimes criticised for being imperialist, racist, sexist and snobbish.

In fact, Enid Blyton's main concern was to tell a good story and she created her plots and characters with this in mind. She portrayed tomboys as well as domesticated girls; George (really Georgina), the tomboy, and Anne, the home-maker, contrast well in the stories about the Famous Five. Jack, who lives with his old grandfather and is always dressed in raggedy things, makes it possible for the three Arnold children who have grown up in a more protected environment to survive on the Secret Island, while Andy, the local fisherman's son, has the knowledge which is vital to the well-being and safety of the Adventurous Four. Both Jack and Andy, although they are only in their early teens, act as surrogate adults. One of Enid Blyton's attractions for young readers is that the adult characters usually play a minor role, behaving in a way dictated by the needs of the plot, whether it is to be the villains of the story or the providers of delicious food.

The Famous Five

The Secret Island

The Adventurous Four

Influences

Enid Blyton's father inspired in her an enthusiasm for natural history and a love of animals, both of which are reflected in her books. George's dog, Timmy, is a major character and counts as one of the Famous Five. Other children have unusual pets, such as Jack's parrot, Kiki, in the Adventure

The Famous Five

The Adventure series

series or Miranda, the monkey, in the books about Barney. She endows animals with human qualities and is very insistent about the importance of being kind to them.

Enid Blyton was also influenced by her childhood reading and describes some of her favourite books in *The Story of My Life* (1952). Among these was a collection of Norse myths which may have inspired one of her most powerful images, the Faraway Tree in *The Enchanted Wood*. The roots of the legendary Norse tree, Yggdrasil, reach down into other worlds while the upper branches of the Faraway Tree take Fanny, Bessie and Jo to a succession of strange countries, and both trees are inhabited by red squirrels who act as go-betweens. She also enjoyed R.M. Ballantyne's *Coral Island*, published in 1858. Authors have been attracted to islands ever since Daniel Defoe wrote *Robinson Crusoe* in 1719 and *The Secret Island* was Blyton's first full-length adventure story while *The Island of Adventure* and *Five on a Treasure Island* are the first titles in two of her most popular series.

The odd one out

In Enid Blyton's stories, good behaviour and honesty are always rewarded while bad behaviour and wrong-doing are punished. This is how young people expect life to be, just as they generally like a story to have a happy ending. *The Six Bad Boys* is rather different from Enid Blyton's other books. The first edition contained a foreword by Basil Henriques, a distinguished Juvenile Court chairman, who praised it for the way in which it shows how six boys, for various reasons, all get into serious trouble. *The Six Bad Boys* makes interesting reading as the problems which cause the boys to commit crimes sadly still exist today, and are far more openly discussed than they were in 1951, when the book was first published.

Although Enid Blyton wrote many different kinds of story, her best known and most popular books today are the nursery stories for younger children, the adventure stories for older children and the school stories which appeal to girls in their early teens.

Nursery Stories

For the very young Enid Blyton wrote stories about toys, animals and fairies that were highly illustrated. One of these, looking rather like a comic-strip story, appeared on the centre pages of each issue of *Sunny Stories* and was no doubt much enjoyed by the youngest members of the family. During World War II, when paper was in short supply, one publisher bought offcuts, small sheets of paper for which there was no other obvious use, and asked Enid Blyton to write stories to make little booklets measuring 7 cm by 15 cm. For these she produced 23 tales of Mary Mouse (now out of print) who looks after the dolls in a dolls' house. Her husband, Whiskers, is the gardener and there are six little mice and a dog.

Mary Mouse

For six-to-eight year olds there were short stories about toys, animals, fairy folk and small children. Most of these have some kind of message; for example, that it doesn't pay to be rude, that it's important to remember things and that, as long as people are kind and honest, it doesn't matter what they look like. There are collections of these stories. Sometimes they are all about the same character, such as Amelia Jane, but in other cases there is a mix as in *Five O'Clock Tales*. These are all good for reading aloud.

Five O'Clock Tales

One of Enid Blyton's most famous creations is Noddy, who lives on his own in Toyland, drives his own car and leads the kind of life that children think they might enjoy. However, Mrs Tubby keeps a motherly eye on him and Big-Ears bosses him about. The Noddy stories were inspired by the brightly coloured illustrations by Harmsen Van Der Beek, a Dutchman. He and Enid Blyton worked closely together on the books with their mix of characters, including toys and pixies and other fantasy folk, all enjoying busy

Noddy

and adventurous lives. After Van Der Beek died in 1953 other artists imitated his style, and the stories continued to appear regularly until Enid Blyton died in 1968.

Mystery and Adventure Stories

The stories about the Secret Seven are mystery stories. The children meet at the house where Janet and Peter live and form a secret society which meets in a garden shed and has passwords. In each book there is a mystery to be solved. The children are alerted by a theft, an unusual happening or a suspicious character lurking in the area. The police welcome the children's help, the parents don't seem to mind them going out at night to tangle with criminals and everyone is pleased with their achievements.

The Secret Seven

The Five Find-Outers, who first appeared in *The Mystery of the Burnt Cottage*, are rather older and use the techniques of the classic detective novel – looking for clues, making a list of suspects and gradually eliminating them – to solve mysteries. They clash with the village policeman, Mr Goon, but their skills are highly admired by the other adult characters, including Police Inspector Jenks. Young readers enjoy all this.

The Mystery of the Burnt Cottage

The Famous Five and the children in the Secret, Barney and Adventure series travel further from home and are often involved in even more dangerous adventures – tracking down smugglers, thieves, kidnappers, spies and other assorted criminals or venturing into alien environments. What is known as the holiday adventure story became very popular in the 1930s and authors had to find ever new variations on the themes of survival and treasure-hunting.

The Secret Island

In *The Secret Island* the three Arnold children, Peggy, Mike and Nora, and their friend, Jack, run away from unkind relations and survive on an island in the middle of a lake until their parents return. Jack knows how to catch fish, snare rabbits and find mushrooms, nuts and blackberries which are good to eat, while Peggy is very domesticated and

The Secret Mountain

makes sure they are warm and well fed. In a later book, *The Secret Mountain*, the children travel out to Africa to look for Mr and Mrs Arnold who have been lost in an air crash, and escape from the anger of the local people by making it appear that they have magically caused a total eclipse of the sun.

While the Famous Five change very little during 21 books, the Barney, Adventure and Secret series have a logi-

The Rockingdown Mystery

cal sequence. In *The Rockingdown Mystery* motherless Barney is searching for his father whom he has never known, and is reunited with him in the fourth book. In *The*

Island of Adventure the children meet super crime-solver Bill Cunningham, whose relationship with their mother develops book by book until, in *The Ship of Adventure*, they decide to marry.

The Island of Adventure

The Ship of Adventure

School Stories

Enid Blyton's first school stories were about Whyteleafe, a co-educational boarding school where the children are very much involved in running things. Such schools were rare in the 1930s but as the stories were first published as serials in *Sunny Stories*, they had to appeal to both boys and girls. Elizabeth Allen, the naughtiest girl, hates the idea of going to school and decides to behave as badly as possible so that she will be sent home. However, before long she realises that Whyteleafe is the best school in the world.

The Naughtiest Girl in the School

School stories were the most popular kind of reading in the early part of the 20th century, but it was the girls who enjoyed them most and they preferred tales about girls-only schools, so St Clare's and Malory Towers are both girls' schools. The O'Sullivan twins at St Clare's and Darrell Rivers at Malory Towers work their way up from being new girls to being chosen as head girls. Apart from the tricks played on the staff and each other, the interest lies in the

St Clare's Malory Towers

changing relationships between the girls, their various problems and in school activities. Darrell Rivers, whose name was inspired by that of Enid Blyton's second husband, Darrell Waters, is a very attractive heroine and one of Blyton's most successful characters. At the end of the series, she and three of her friends are looking forward to going to university. In the later books about Malory Towers Enid Blyton showed that she was aware of the changes in society after World War II which made it more likely that girls would go on to higher education and enjoy satisfying careers.

Still popular today

Because the plots, characters and style of Enid Blyton's books are simple and straightforward, they have survived the passing of time, and do not seem old-fashioned in the way that other books published before 1960 may do. Readers are so anxious to find out what happens next that they don't notice the lack of televisions and computers, nor that the lavish descriptions of food don't mention fish fingers, pizzas, pasta or yoghurts. One great attraction is that the children have more freedom to roam than they do today. When Enid Blyton was writing, the local environment was a much safer place for children, and even parents who liked to know what their children were up to, were happy to let them go off walking, cycling or even camping on their own.

Some of Enid Blyton's books have been updated to make them acceptable to modern tastes. For example, the golliwogs in the Noddy books have been replaced and some *Noddy* of the female characters have been made more positive and independent. Some words such as 'gay' and 'queer' have changed their meaning and have been replaced too. However, there are still many old copies around, even if they are in a rather tattered and well-read condition, so it's possible to come across the books as they were originally written.

Today there are film and television versions of some of the books. Audio and video tapes are readily accessible and there are Blyton websites on the Internet. Nursery furnishings and equipment, and games and jigsaw puzzles are based on popular Blyton characters. A few of the series have been continued by other writers. The German language sequels to the stories about Malory Towers have never been *Malory Towers* published in English, but new stories about the Famous *Famous Five* Five, written in French by Claude Voilier, were translated into English in the early 1980s. More recently Anne Digby has written books that continue the story of the Naughtiest *The Naughtiest Girl* Girl.

Nobody knows just how many books Enid Blyton wrote, probably over seven hundred, with many different publishers. She wrote many kinds of stories – fantasy, family, adventure, school – about the things she enjoyed and knew about., Now, over a hundred years after she was born, there are few people who have not heard of Enid Blyton.

Sheila Ray

2000

Enid in 1951, in front of a bookcase that contained all the books she had written at that time. Up to 300 more were added before she died.

Bibliography

This is a small selection of Enid Blyton's books, arranged in order of publication. Many of them are the first in a series of books about the same characters; further titles in the series are given below each entry. The second publisher and date given indicate an edition that is currently in print; 'o.p.' means the book is out of print and not currently available new in bookshops, although you may find copies in charity shops.

Adventures of the Wishing Chair
Newnes 1937; Mammoth 1992

A magic chair takes Peter, Mollie and Chinky the pixie on strange adventures during which they meet giants, goblins, witches and other unusual creatures.

Further titles in this series: The Wishing Chair Again

Heyo, Brer Rabbit! Tales of Brer Rabbit and his Friends

Newnes 1937; as *Brer Rabbit and the Potato Fight* HarperCollins 1998

Stories of Brer Rabbit, the trickster, were traditional African tales brought by slaves to the southern states of America and the West Indies. They were first written down by Joel Chandler Harris and published as the stories of Uncle Remus in 1880. Enid Blyton simplified the style and the language, and emphasised the humour of the tales.

The Secret Island

Blackwell 1938; filmscript novelisation HarperCollins 1998

This was Enid Blyton's first holiday adventure story, in which four children live a Robinson Crusoe kind of life on an island in an English lake.

Further titles in this series: The Secret of Spiggy Holes, The Secret Mountain, The Secret of Killimooin, The Secret of Moon Castle

Mr Galliano's Circus

Newnes 1938 o.p.

In the 1930s circuses were popular entertainment; we now have very different ideas about how animals should be

treated, although Enid Blyton was always careful to empha-
sise the importance of kindness to animals. Jimmy Brown
loves them and when his father, a carpenter, joins a circus, he
manages to train his dog, Lucky, to perform in the ring. He
makes friends with Lotta who also has a successful circus act.

*Further titles in this series: Hurrah for the Circus!, Circus Days
Again*

The Enchanted Wood

Newnes 1939; Mammoth 1992

Bessie, Fanny and Jo move to a cottage in the country and
discover the Faraway Tree in a nearby wood. They make
friends with the woodland folk and are taken up the tree to
visit a succession of wonderful lands. This is the Enid Blyton
book many adults remember most clearly from childhood.

*Further titles in this series: The Magic Faraway Tree, The Folk of the
Faraway Tree*

Naughty Amelia Jane

Newnes 1939; Mammoth 1992

Amelia Jane is a doll who almost always behaves badly.
The other nursery toys frequently get their revenge and

Amelia Jane promises to turn over a new leaf, but her good intentions tend to be very temporary.

Further titles in this series: Amelia Jane Again, More about Amelia Jane

The Adventurous Four
Blackwell 1940; HarperCollins 1998

Although Enid Blyton's books reflect life in Britain as it was at the time they were written, she rarely mentions events of historical importance. *The Adventurous Four* is one of the exceptions. The children are up against Nazis, who have established a submarine base on an island off the Scottish coast. Needless to say, they outwit the enemy and carry important information back to the British authorities.

Further titles in this series: The Adventurous Four Again

The Naughtiest Girl in the School
Newnes 1940; Hodder 1999

Elizabeth Allen hates being at Whyteleaf, a very progressive co-educational school. She decides to be as naughty as possible so that she will be sent home.

Further titles in this series: The Naughtiest Girl Again, The Naughtiest Girl is a Monitor

Five O'Clock Tales

Methuen 1941; Mammoth 1993

This is one of Enid Blyton's many story collections for younger children.

The Twins at St Clare's

Methuen 1941; Mammoth 2000

Patricia and Isabel O'Sullivan have been head girls at their first school and are full of their own importance when they arrive at St Clare's as first formers. Now they have to adapt to being amongst the youngest girls. They only once make use of the fact that they are identical twins, but have fun, make good friends and learn how to get on with other people.

Further titles in this series: The O'Sullivan Twins, Summer Term at St Clare's, The Second Form at St Clare's, Claudine at St Clare's, Fifth Formers at St Clare's; two further titles (written by Pamela Cox) have now been added to the series – Third Form at St Clare's and Sixth Form at St Clare's.

Five on a Treasure Island

Hodder and Stoughton 1942; Hodder 1995

In this first of the Famous Five books, Julian, Dick and

Anne meet their cousin George (short for Georgina) and her dog Timmy, and help to restore the family fortunes. Aunt Fanny is kind but Uncle Quentin is a bad-tempered scientist who often makes things difficult. Julian regards himself as the leader, but George can hold her own. Anne, the youngest, behaves more like girls were expected to behave in the 1940s.

Further titles in this series: Five Go Adventuring Again, Five Run Away Together, Five Go to Smuggler's Top, Five Go Off in a Caravan, Five on Kirrin Island Again, Five Go Off to Camp, Five Get into Trouble, Five Fall into Adventure, Five on a Hike Together, Five have a Wonderful Time, Five Go Down to the Sea, Five Go to Mystery Moor, Five Have Plenty of Fun, Five on a Secret Trail, Five Go to Billycock Hill, Five Get into a Fix, Five on Finniston Farm, Five Go to Demon's Rocks, Five Have a Mystery to Solve, Five are Together Again

The Land of Far Beyond

Methuen 1942; Element 1998

Enid Blyton retold many Bible stories. This is her retelling of John Bunyan's *Pilgrim's Progress*, which was one of the most popular books amongst children for long after it was first published in 1678. Although some children still received it as a present or Sunday school prize in the 1940s, very few were able to get through it. So Enid Blyton decided to write the same kind of story in a way that would appeal to them.

Mary Mouse and the Doll's House
Brockhampton 1942 o.p.

The first book about Mary Mouse and her family, and how they came to look after the dolls in the doll's house. If you find one of these in good condition, treasure it!

Further titles in this series: More Adventures of Mary Mouse, Little Mary Mouse Again, Hallo Little Mary Mouse, Mary Mouse and her Family, Here Comes Mary Mouse Again, How do you do, Mary Mouse?, We Do Love Mary Mouse, Welcome Mary Mouse, Hurrah for Mary Mouse, A Prize for Mary Mouse, Mary Mouse and her Bicycle, Mary Mouse and the Noah's Ark, Mary Mouse to the Rescue, Mary Mouse in Nursery Rhyme Land, A Day with Mary Mouse, Mary Mouse and the Garden Party, Mary Mouse Goes to the Fair, Mary Mouse has a Wonderful Idea, Mary Mouse Goes to Sea, Mary Mouse Goes Out for the Day, Fun with Mary Mouse, Mary Mouse and the Little Donkey

Shadow, the Sheep Dog

Newnes 1942 o.p.

Although Enid Blyton was very fond of animals and wrote factual books about them as well as including them in her stories, this is a rarity – a full-length book written from the animal's point of view. It tells the story of Shadow from the time he is a puppy until he is brave and strong enough to rescue a lamb that is being attacked by an eagle.

The Mystery of the Burnt Cottage

Methuen 1943; Mammoth 1995

This is the first mystery for the Find-Outers, Bets, Pip, Larry, Daisy and Fatty. Peterswood, the village where the children live, seems to be based on the village of Bourne End in Buckinghamshire, and is one of the few places used by Enid Blyton that can be positively identified.

Further titles in this series: The Mystery of the Disappearing Cat, The Mystery of the Secret Room, The Mystery of the Spiteful Letters, The Mystery of the Missing Necklace, The Mystery of the Hidden House, The Mystery of the Pantomime Cat, The Mystery of the Invisible Thief, The Mystery of the Vanished Prince, The Mystery of the Strange Bundle, The Mystery of Holly Lane, The Mystery of Tally-Ho Cottage,

The Mystery of the Missing Man, The Mystery of the Strange Message,
The Mystery of Banshee Towers

The Boy Next Door
Newnes 1944; as *The Riddle of the Boy Next Door* HarperCollins 1997

Robin hopes that a boy his own age will move into the empty house next door, but when Kit arrives there is a great mystery surrounding him.

The Island of Adventure
Macmillan 1944; Macmillan 1998

This is the first book in the Adventure series, in which Jack and Lucy-Ann, who are orphans, and Dinah and Philip Mannering, whose mother is widowed, and Kiki the parrot, with a little help from Bill Cunningham, successfully tackle a variety of criminals. In a review of *The Sea of Adventure* in 1948, one critic wrote, 'What hope has a band of desperate men against four children?'

Further titles in this series: The Castle of Adventure, The Valley of Adventure, The Sea of Adventure, The Mountain of Adventure, The Ship of Adventure, The Circus of Adventure, The River of Adventure

The Caravan Family

Lutterworth 1945; Mammoth 1997

The first book about Mike, Belinda and Ann who live in all sorts of different homes and go on various types of holiday.

Further titles in this series: The Saucy Jane Family, The Pole Star Family, The Seaside Family, The Buttercup Farm Family, The Queen Elizabeth Family

First Term at Malory Towers

Methuen 1946; Mammoth 2000

Darrell Rivers arrives at Malory Towers, keen and enthusiastic but aware that school life is likely to be very different from how it is described in school stories. She makes good friends, works hard and has fun.

Further titles in this series: The Second Form at Malory Towers, Third Year at Malory Towers, Upper Fourth at Malory Towers, In the Fifth at Malory Towers, Last Term at Malory Towers

Little Noddy Goes to Toyland

Sampson Low 1949; as *Noddy Goes to Toyland* HarperCollins 1996

Noddy is Enid Blyton's most famous creation, and hardest to miss. As well as being the central character in 24 books,

Background: Illustration for First Term at Malory Towers

models of him in his car are often found outside super-markets so that small children can join him for a ride.

Further titles in this series: Hurrah for Little Noddy, Noddy and his Car, Here Comes Noddy Again!, Well Done Noddy, Noddy Goes to School, Noddy at the Seaside, Noddy Gets into Trouble, Noddy and the Magic Rubber, You Funny Little Noddy, Noddy Meets Father Christmas, Noddy and Tessie Bear, Be Brave Little Noddy, Noddy and the Bumpy-Dog, Do Look Out Noddy!, You're a Good Friend Noddy!, Noddy Has an Adventure, Noddy Goes to Sea, Noddy and the Bunkey, Cheer Up Little Noddy, Noddy Goes to the Fair, Mr Plod and Little Noddy, Noddy and the Tootles, Noddy and the Aeroplane

The Rockingdown Mystery
Collins 1949; Armada 1990

All the books in the Barney series have something beginning with 'R' in the title. In this first book, Diana and Roger and their young cousin, Snubby, and Snubby's dog, Loony, meet Barney, a mysterious boy who lives the life of a capable and independent loner.

Further titles in this series: The Rilloby Fair Mystery, The Ring O'Bells Mystery, The Rubadub Mystery, The Rat-a-tat Mystery, The Ragamuffin Mystery

The Secret Seven
Brockhampton 1949; Hodder 1996

The stories about the Secret Seven – Janet, Peter, George, Pam, Barbara, Colin and Jack – were written for slightly younger children than those about the Famous Five. The children are younger and their adventures take place in a more domestic environment, based in a garden shed. The idea of a secret society begins to appeal to children when they are about seven or eight and want to be more independent of their parents.

Further titles in this series: Secret Seven Adventure, Well Done Secret Seven, Secret Seven on the Trail, Go Ahead Secret Seven, Good Work Secret Seven, Secret Seven Win Through, Three Cheers Secret Seven, Secret Seven Mystery, Puzzle for the Secret Seven, Secret Seven Fireworks, Good Old Secret Seven, Shock for the Secret Seven, Look Out Secret Seven, Fun for the Secret Seven

The Six Bad Boys
Lutterworth 1951; Award 1999

This was the last of Enid Blyton's books to break new ground. Six boys set up their headquarters in the cellar of a partly ruined terraced house and become involved in a life of petty crime.

Enid Blyton's Adventure Treasury
Hodder 1999

Complied by Mary Cadogan and Norman Wright

After her death, many of Enid Blyton's stories appeared in new formats. *The Adventure Treasury*, published in the last year of the 20th century, is a celebration of the author who dominated children's books for much of it. Helen Cresswell contributes a foreword and Gillian Baverstock a short memoir of her mother. It is illustrated throughout and includes extracts from her most famous books and short stories. There are coloured reproductions of book jackets, covers of *Sunny Stories* and spin-offs such as jigsaw puzzles and card games, while the endpapers illustrate the Secret Seven and Famous Five board games.

If you want to find out more about Enid Blyton, her official biography is: *Enid Blyton: The Biography* by Barbara Stoney (Hodder 1997). You could also look for Enid Blyton websites on the Internet.

Acknowledgements

Quotations and information from: *The Story of My Life* by Enid Blyton; quotations from Enid Blyton's letters to Dr Peter McKellar during research for his book, *Imagination and Thinking* (pub 1957).

Grateful acknowledgements to: Barbara Stoney, author of *Enid Blyton, The Biography*; Tony Summerfield and Brian Stewart, authors of *The Enid Blyton Dossier*.

A plaque on the wall of Elfin Cottage, 83 Shortland Road, where Enid lived from 1925–1929.